Original title:
In the Aftermath

Copyright © 2024 Swan Charm
All rights reserved.

Author: Lan Donne
ISBN HARDBACK: 978-9916-79-134-9
ISBN PAPERBACK: 978-9916-79-135-6
ISBN EBOOK: 978-9916-79-136-3

Unholy Testaments and Sacred Dreams

In shadows deep where whispers creep,
Lies the heart's lament and silent weep.
Beneath the gaze of stars so bright,
We ponder truths obscured by night.

With faith unshaken, we tread the path,
Through storms of doubt and reckless wrath.
For every tear that stains the ground,
A sacred dream in hope is found.

Yet voices clash within the soul,
Desires fierce that take their toll.
Unholy testaments inscribed in pain,
Echo through the vastness, like falling rain.

In quiet prayer, we seek the light,
To mend the rifts and end the fight.
For in the void, where shadows loom,
A glimmer shines, dispelling gloom.

Awake, arise, embrace the grace,
In every heart, the sacred place.
Though trials bend our weary knees,
With faith, we rise, our spirits free.

Ashes to Angels in Silent Rest

From ashes rise the souls so bright,
Transcending pain to find the light.
In quiet nights, their whispers flow,
A testament of love we know.

They dance on winds, in grace they soar,
With every tear, they heal the sore.
In silent rest, they guard our dreams,
In sacred peace, their spirit gleams.

With faith we tread through darkest hours,
Transformed by grace, we bloom like flowers.
The bond of heart, forever strong,
In unity, we sing our song.

Through trials faced, the heart does mend,
In each embrace, we find a friend.
Ashes to angels, love refined,
In silent rest, we are aligned.

The Message Carried by the Winds of Change

In whispers soft, the breezes call,
They carry dreams and truths for all.
Through rustling leaves and skies so wide,
The message flows, our hearts as guide.

With every gust, a chance to heal,
The past released, our wounds conceal.
New paths emerge, in faith we stride,
As winds of change become our guide.

In every heart, a spark ignites,
Awakening hope, reaching new heights.
Embrace the shift, let go of fear,
The winds of change draw ever near.

In unity, we stand as one,
The battle fought, the victory won.
With open arms, we greet the dawn,
The message carried, life reborn.

Pilgrimage through the Depths of Brokenness

An odyssey through shadows deep,
With weary hearts, we mourn and weep.
Yet every tear, a sacred trust,
In brokenness, we find what's just.

With every step, our burdens share,
A journey marked by love and care.
Through valleys low, the spirit soars,
In every crack, the light restores.

With faith as compass, onward tread,
Through trials faced, our spirits led.
In brokenness, we learn to see,
The strength in unity, love's decree.

Resilience blooms in the darkest night,
Emerging souls, embracing light.
The pilgrimage reveals the grace,
In depths of hurt, we find our place.

Shadows of the Forgotten Faith

In shadows cast by doubt's embrace,
The echoes linger, seeking grace.
Through whispered prayers, the faithful weep,
In forgotten halls where silence sleeps.

Yet hope ignites, a flicker small,
Within the heart, a sacred call.
Though trials may dim the brightest flame,
In shadows deep, we share His name.

From ashes rise the stories lost,
In every burden, we count the cost.
Through darkest nights, the stars align,
In shadows cast, the light will shine.

United in faith, our spirits soar,
With every hymn, we seek restore.
In shadows, love will find a way,
The forgotten faith will lead the day.

Blooming from the Barrenness

In deserts deep where shadows creep,
Hope's seed is sown, though spirits weep.
With gentle rain and sun's embrace,
New life springs forth in barren space.

Amidst the thorns, the flowers rise,
A testament to faith's sweet prize.
From cracks in stone, green shoots find light,
In darkest nights, there shines a bright.

The whispers of the wind proclaim,
The beauty found in trials' flame.
Through storms and drought, we seek His grace,
In every heart, His love we trace.

Each petal soft, each fragrance sweet,
A pilgrimage upon our feet.
Through barren lands, we'll walk in trust,
In God's design, we find what's just.

So let us bloom where we are lost,
For in our rise, we pay the cost.
With every prayer, a seed of gold,
In faith we stand, in hope we hold.

The Seraph's Lament

High above in realms divine,
The seraphs sing, their voices fine.
Yet one weeps in the light's embrace,
For love denied in endless grace.

With wings spread wide, they dance in spheres,
But one is lost amidst the tears.
In silent prayer, a heart does sigh,
For the fallen souls who long to fly.

Each note they play, a sorrowed sound,
For those who walk on hollow ground.
In radiant light, they call our name,
Yet still our hearts are bound in shame.

Beneath the veil of earthly strife,
They long to share eternal life.
In every teardrop, hope is spun,
The lament echoes, 'We are one.'

The seraph's heart, though pure and bright,
Still bears the weight of endless nights.
For every soul that turns away,
Their song of love shall ever stay.

Morning Star Over the Abyss

In the silence of the night so deep,
A star descends, its light to keep.
It breaks the darkness, whispers soft,
Bringing hope to souls aloft.

From shadows thick the dawn does break,
In trembling hearts, new hopes awake.
The morning star, with radiant gleam,
Awakens faith, ignites the dream.

Upon the edge of endless night,
It casts a glow, a path so bright.
Each heartbeat echoes, love bestowed,
A guiding light on weary road.

When burdens wear, and spirits strain,
The morning star will ease the pain.
Its gentle rays, a balm so pure,
In every trial, we shall endure.

With trusted light, our fears allay,
In faith we rise, we seek the way.
For in the void, His light will last,
The morning star, our shadows passed.

The Forgotten Psalms of the Fallen

In whispered tones, their voices fade,
The psalms of hearts once unafraid.
Forgotten songs, in silence drown,
Yet in each beat, they wear a crown.

From ashes rise, the embers glow,
Reminders of the love we owe.
In every tear, a story shared,
In every prayer, the lost are bared.

Through darkened veils, their echoes stay,
A haunting grace that lights the way.
In shadows long, they search for peace,
In every soul, their hymn won't cease.

For in the night where sorrow reigns,
The fallen sing of love's sweet chains.
Their psalms of hope, though faintly heard,
In hearts ignited by each word.

Let not forgotten voices die,
For in their songs, we learn to fly.
Together rise, in faith we stand,
The fallen's psalms, forever grand.

The Path of Return

In the stillness of the night,
Soul's whispers call me home.
Each step upon the sacred ground,
Guides me where the shadows roam.

Far beyond the hills of doubt,
Faith's gentle light does shine.
With every breath, I seek the truth,
The heart that beats divine.

Worn are the shoes of the wayfarer,
Mud from trials that I tread.
Yet, on this path of return,
I find the love once fed.

Love's embrace, it draws me near,
To the altar of the past.
Forgive my wanderings and fears,
Let this journey hold steadfast.

In unity, I raise my hands,
To the heavens far and bright.
For in the path of return,
I walk towards eternal light.

Ashes of the Unheard

Whispers in the silent void,
Echoes of the lost refrain.
Hearts that bear the weight of night,
With no voice to speak their pain.

In forgotten corners lie,
Ashes of the prayers unsaid.
To the heavens carry them,
Where souls no longer dread.

Glimmers of hope flicker faint,
Like stars in a darker sky.
In the stillness, faith remains,
To the unseen, we rely.

Beneath the ashes, embers glow,
A truth that yearns to be free.
In the silence of the unheard,
Awaits a new decree.

Lifted by the winds of peace,
Let their voices rise anew.
From the ashes of the unheard,
A chorus breaks through.

The Gospel According to Silence

In the quiet heart of prayer,
Whispers of the soul arise.
Not in shouts, but softest breath,
Does the deeper wisdom lie.

Each moment still, a sacred word,
In silence, truths unfold.
Listen closely; the Spirit speaks,
In tones of grace retold.

Where chatter drowns the tender voice,
Seek refuge in the calm.
For silence carries mysteries,
That wrap the heart in balm.

Let the echoes of the past,
Be woven into today.
In the sacred hush of life,
The gospel leads the way.

So, bow your head and listen well,
To the stillness all around.
In the gospel of true silence,
Divinity is found.

The Last Steps of a Wandering Faith

The road winds through fields of doubt,
A journey long and wide.
Each step weighs down the weary heart,
Yet faith is my guide.

Footprints etched in sacred sand,
Tell tales of battles fought.
In the twilight, I search my soul,
For the lessons love has taught.

With every breath, I release the past,
And hold the light of grace.
For in the last steps of wandering,
I stumble towards His face.

Morning breaks, a brand-new dawn,
Hope flickers through the night.
In the arms of whispered prayers,
I find my heart's true sight.

The last steps lead me home at last,
To where the spirit flows.
In the dance of a wandering faith,
Eternal love bestows.

Grace Amidst the Desolation

In the silence, whispers flow,
Hearts in anguish, yet we know.
Through the darkness, love will shine,
Embracing souls, forever divine.

When the night seems everlong,
Faith will guide us, steady, strong.
Hope a beacon, burning bright,
Leading us towards the light.

In the struggles, grace will bloom,
Filling spaces, quelling gloom.
From the ashes, beauty rise,
A testament to the skies.

Each tear a prayer, softly said,
Healing journeys, paths we tread.
With each heartbeat, love will grow,
Woven in the good we sow.

Through despair, a song will play,
Carried on the winds of day.
In the desolation's grip,
We find the strength to rise and live.

The Altar of Forgotten Prayers

Upon the altar, dust will lay,
Echoes of what we wished to say.
In the shadows, hopes remain,
Yearning hearts, quiet pain.

Candles flicker, dreams dispersed,
In silence, the spirit's thirst.
Each whispered word, a gentle plea,
To the heavens, set us free.

Gathered here with love entwined,
Memories lost, yet intertwined.
Yet in stillness, grace abides,
With open arms, the heart confides.

Buried deep, the prayers call,
In the stillness, hear them all.
From forgotten, new will bloom,
In the light, dispelling gloom.

As we kneel, our burdens bare,
Cleansed by love, we find our prayer.
In the echoes of the night,
We find our way, guided by light.

Veils of Light in the Shadowed Valley

In the valley, shadows play,
Veils of light guide our way.
Through the murk and the unknown,
Heartfelt whispers, softly grown.

Each step carries hopes anew,
In the dark, we find the view.
Light illuminates the path,
Dispelling all the aftermath.

With courage born of faith's embrace,
We walk boldly, filled with grace.
Through the trials, hearts align,
Bound in love, eternally thine.

In the shadows, peace will reign,
Transforming sorrow into gain.
With every tear, a promise made,
In the light, choices laid.

Hope arises, souls unite,
In the valley's gentle light.
Together we shall journey far,
Guided always by the star.

Transcendence Beyond the Ashes

From the ashes, life will spring,
In the ruins, birds will sing.
With each flame that flickers low,
New beginnings start to grow.

In the quiet, strength we find,
Fire burns, yet love is kind.
Through the loss, we learn to rise,
In our hearts, the spirit flies.

Hope emerges from the strife,
In the struggle, blooms new life.
Connected in our shared despair,
Together woven, hearts laid bare.

Transcendence calls us to believe,
In every trial, we receive.
From the shadows, light will blaze,
Guiding us through life's maze.

Rebirth chorus in the dawn,
With each heartbeat, we walk on.
Through the ashes, love will soar,
In the end, we are restored.

Revelations from the Wounded Earth

In silence, the earth whispers deep,
A tale of wounds, a sorrow to keep.
The mountains groan beneath the weight,
While rivers weep for a kinder fate.

Beneath the stars, hope starts to rise,
In shadows cast by the darkest skies.
Nature's cries echo through the night,
In healing hands, we find the light.

The flowers bloom in defiant grace,
Their colors bright, a sacred space.
From ashes of pain, new life will spring,
Each heartbeat hums, a sacred hymn.

We walk the path of ancient fears,
Through tears and trials, through laugh and jeers.
Yet faith abounds in trials steep,
The promise of dawn, a joy to reap.

So hear the call, O mighty friend,
In every wound, a chance to mend.
For from the earth, our spirits learn,
The cycle of life, the fire's burn.

The Pilgrim's Path through Broken Dreams

With weary feet, the pilgrim strides,
Through shattered hopes, where darkness hides.
Each step a prayer, a silent plea,
For guidance through lost reverie.

The road is thick with thorns and fears,
Yet every sorrow, a song appears.
In broken dreams, we find our way,
A tapestry rich, both night and day.

The stars above, like candles shine,
Reminding hearts of the divine.
Through winding paths of doubt and ache,
The soul awakens, a dawn to make.

In every stumble, a lesson dear,
A whisper of love, a voice so near.
Together we rise, hand in hand,
On the pilgrim's path, we understand.

So carry forth, dear wanderer bold,
In every story, a truth to hold.
With faith as our map and love our guide,
We tread the path with hearts open wide.

Resilience of the Faithful Heart

In the depths of night, when shadows creep,
The faithful heart does not lose sleep.
For hope is a lantern, burning bright,
Guiding through struggle, embracing light.

Amidst the storms and raging seas,
The heart finds strength in whispered pleas.
Each sorrow speaks of a greater plan,
In every trial, a faithful hand.

The fire within never fades away,
It dances amidst the night and day.
With courage sewn in every seam,
The faithful heart holds onto dreams.

Through valleys low and mountains high,
The spirit soars on wings of sighs.
For every tear that falls like rain,
A flower blooms from the seeds of pain.

Resilience lies in love's pure grace,
A sacred bond, a warm embrace.
In trials fierce, the soul departs,
To find the strength within our hearts.

Candles Flicker in the Gloom

In darkest rooms where shadows dwell,
Candles flicker, casting spells.
Each flame a hope, a soothing balm,
In whispered prayers, we find our calm.

The world may spin in chaos loud,
Yet in that flicker, a promise proud.
For against the night, the light will fight,
Defying sorrow with its might.

As winter's chill grips earth so tight,
The candles glow, igniting night.
In every flicker, a story told,
Of love and faith, both brave and bold.

Together we gather, hand in hand,
Illuminating the weary land.
In darkness deep, our spirits soar,
With every candle, we seek for more.

So let us hold our flames alight,
In unity, we conquer fright.
For in the gloom, where shadows play,
Candles flicker, guiding the way.

Footprints in the Wastes

In barren lands where silence reigns,
The weary walk through shadows' chains.
Yet in each step, Your light remains,
Guiding hearts through bitter pains.

Footprints soft on desert sand,
Whispers grace where hope can stand.
Your mercy flows, a gentle hand,
Reviving dreams in this dry land.

Each soul a vessel, lost yet found,
Through trials steep, Your love is bound.
In wanderlust, we quest around,
For solace in the hallowed ground.

With every sigh, a prayer ascends,
To You, O Lord, our journey bends.
In the wastes, Your promise lends,
A path of light that never ends.

So let us walk, united still,
With faith aglow, and iron will.
In footsteps left, Your purpose fulfill,
In barren wastes, our hearts You fill.

The Quiet Sacrifice of Nightfall

As daylight fades to twilight's grace,
The stars awaken, take their place.
In silence deep, we find Your face,
In every shadow, love we trace.

The moon, a witness to our plight,
Cantatas sung in softest light.
Each whisper cloaked in velvet night,
Bears witness to the purest fight.

Through gentle dreams, our souls ascend,
To realms where time and sorrow blend.
In night's embrace, we make amends,
For every heart that love defends.

With every star that lights the sky,
We cast our burdens, let them fly.
In night, we seek the reasons why,
Like flowers blooming, we shall vie.

In stillness lies a hidden gift,
Your grace bestowed, a holy lift.
As darkness fades, our spirits drift,
In quiet ways, our hearts You scribe.

Beneath the Weight of Broken Dreams

In shattered hopes, we lay our heads,
With heavy hearts and silent threads.
Yet in the ruins, a voice spreads,
A promise where the spirit leads.

Each dream a seed, once bold and bright,
Now buried deep within the night.
Yet still, Your hand brings forth the light,
To mend the wounds and wrongs ignite.

Through trials fierce, like storms that rage,
Our stories penned on time's old page.
With faith restored, we turn the stage,
For all our fears, a blessed wage.

In solace found, we rise anew,
With each breath taken, faith breaks through.
For in the dark, Your promise grew,
In broken dreams, we find what's true.

So lift our eyes to skies once grey,
To find the dawn of a brand new day.
For every tear that fell away,
A rainbow forms where shadows play.

Soul's Journey through the Marrow

Through marrow deep, our spirits sigh,
In whispers soft, we seek the high.
With every pulse, we wonder why,
In shadows cast, our hopes do fly.

From depths unknown, the heartbeats call,
In sacred rhythm, forth we crawl.
With every rise, we fear the fall,
But in Your presence, love enthralls.

Each stumble leads us to the light,
In darkness, we embrace the fight.
For every tear that dims our sight,
Your grace restores the endless night.

The marrow's truth, a sacred song,
In verses bold, we find the strong.
With every breath, we all belong,
In unity, our hearts prolong.

So let us journey, hand in hand,
Through deep and wide, o'er shifting sand.
In faith, our souls together stand,
To reach the promise of Your land.

In the Wake of the Divine

In stillness, grace descends anew,
Heaven's light in morning's dew.
Hearts uplifted, spirits rise,
In the hush, divine replies.

Echoes of a sacred song,
In every soul, we all belong.
Through trials faced, our faith ignites,
With love that guides, we seek the heights.

In the wake of caring hands,
Life unfolds as mercy spans.
Beneath the stars, our path is clear,
In unity, we persevere.

Trust the promise of the dawn,
With every breath, we carry on.
In prayers whispered, hopes take flight,
Together, we embrace the light.

The heart knows where the spirit leads,
In every moment, truth proceeds.
In gratitude, we stand as one,
In the wake of what's begun.

Threads of Promise in the Dusk

As daylight fades, a promise gleams,
In twilight's hush, we stitch our dreams.
Each thread we weave, a prayer in time,
In sacred hush, our souls align.

Stars emerge, with stories bright,
Guiding us through the velvet night.
In quiet grace, we find our strength,
In love's embrace, we journey length.

The dusk unveils what's meant to be,
In whispers soft, we hear the plea.
In every shadow, light is sown,
In togetherness, we have grown.

Threads of faith entwined in peace,
In unity, our fears release.
Beneath the heavens, souls entwine,
In the twilight, love's design.

To dream again as darkness falls,
In the silence, the spirit calls.
With every heartbeat, trust our fate,
In the dusk, we contemplate.

Scars of Sacred Temples

Beneath the surface, stories hide,
In every fracture, love abides.
The sacred temples bear their pain,
Through trials faced, the soul remains.

Each scar a mark, a path to grace,
In vulnerability, we embrace.
In strength reclaimed, we rise anew,
Through brokenness, we find what's true.

From ashes rise, a spirit bold,
With every tear, a tale is told.
Through suffering, the heart expands,
In healing hands, our essence stands.

The light shines through each fragile crack,
In every heart, love brings us back.
With reverence, we honor pain,
As sacred whisper drives the gain.

In temples built on trust and faith,
We bind the wounds, embrace the wraith.
With open hearts, we journey on,
In the scars, new worlds are drawn.

Celestial Whispers After the Storm

After the tempest, calm returns,
In stillness, the heart yearns.
Celestial whispers fill the air,
In gentle tones, a soothing prayer.

The skies unveil a brighter hue,
As hope emerges, fresh and true.
In the silence, wisdom flows,
From every trial, the spirit grows.

Through storms endured, we gather strength,
In unity, we find our length.
With every raindrop, light bestowed,
In every heart, a love that glowed.

Celestial orbs that watch from high,
Bathe us gently, as we sigh.
Each breath a pledge, a vow to keep,
In gratitude, our souls will leap.

In whispers soft, the truth we seek,
In every moment, we feel the meek.
After the storm, let love reform,
In warmth of grace, our spirits swarm.

Vestiges of Light from the Depth

In shadows deep where silence dwells,
A whisper calls, a soft farewell.
Through veils of night, a glow ignites,
A trail of grace, from lost to sights.

With every tear that grace does sew,
In depths of grief, the spirits grow.
Each sorrow holds a sacred seed,
A promise born from faith's true lead.

Among the ruins, hearts will mend,
As echoes of the past transcend.
Light shines through cracks of broken dreams,
In depths of night, the spirit beams.

The soul remembers love's embrace,
As vestiges of light we trace.
In darkest hour, hope reclaims,
The depth of love, the spark remains.

The Communion of the Lost and Found

In gathering shadows, we take our place,
The lost souls wander, seeking grace.
In whispered prayers, our voices blend,
A sacred bond, where hearts transcend.

The fragments scattered, yet intertwined,
In moments shared, the light we find.
With every story, a thread anew,
In faith's embrace, we are made true.

Through trials faced, the path unveils,
In unity's warmth, the spirit sails.
In humble hearts, our burdens shared,
The light of love, eternally bared.

Together we heal, together we rise,
In the communion of compassionate ties.
From lost to found, our spirits align,
In every struggle, our grace will shine.

The Vision of Celestial Renewal

Awake, O heart, to the dawn anew,
In celestial glow, all eyes in view.
A vision bright, where hope finds wing,
In every soul, a song to sing.

The heavens weep, then grant their light,
Transforming shadows, igniting night.
In sacred air, the whispers rise,
From earth to heaven, a sweet reprise.

With every breath, a chance to start,
To weave the dreams that dwell in heart.
A tapestry born from love's embrace,
In unity's thread, we find our place.

Let grace renew our weary gaze,
In every moment, ignite the blaze.
The vision waits, with arms outspread,
To lift the weary, to guide the dead.

The Tapestry of Tomorrow's Hope

In threads of time, the future's spun,
A tapestry where dreams are won.
Each color bright, a life's embrace,
In every stitch, a sacred place.

The weaver's hand, with gentle grace,
Shapes destinies, finds each lost face.
With love as guide, our hearts align,
In every challenge, the stars will shine.

Through trials faced, a portrait grows,
A map of faith, as sunlight shows.
Tomorrow's hope is born today,
In each surrender, it finds its way.

Let us unite, both far and near,
With hearts as one, we conquer fear.
The tapestry glows, in night's embrace,
A radiant vision, a sacred space.

Renewed in Brokenness

In whispers soft, His grace descends,
To mend the hearts that faith transcends.
From ashes low, we rise anew,
In brokenness, His love breaks through.

The shards of pain, a sacred art,
He binds the wounds, heals every heart.
In humble trust, we find our song,
In brokenness, we still belong.

Each tear we shed, a prayer unfolds,
In silent nights, His truth we hold.
The light that shines from shattered dreams,
Reveals the hope in darkest streams.

With every breath, we seek the dawn,
Through trials faced, we carry on.
In every struggle, faith is sown,
Renewed in grace, we're never alone.

So lift your hearts from depths of grief,
In brokenness, we find relief.
In every fracture, love's embrace,
We rise again, renewed in grace.

Covenant of the Unsung

Beneath the stars, the unsung hymn,
A promise held, a light so dim.
In humble hearts, His truth we find,
A covenant, eternal and kind.

Through silent vows and whispered prayers,
A sacred bond, in quiet layers.
Though unseen faces bear the weight,
They walk in grace, their fate, our fate.

In every step, their echoes call,
From hidden trails, they rise and fall.
With faith unyielding, dreams take flight,
In shadows deep, they seek the light.

For every tear, a story flows,
Of courage found where no one knows.
A tapestry of love each day,
In lives unsung, His grace holds sway.

The bond of hearts, though often veiled,
In unity, the truth prevailed.
In quiet strength, the faithful stand,
A covenant held, hand in hand.

Refuge in the Embers of Sorrow

In darkest nights where shadows creep,
We find a refuge, safe and deep.
The embers glow with warmth and light,
In sorrow's grip, we hold on tight.

Though storms may rage, and tempests roar,
We seek the peace that's ours, for sure.
With every wound, the heart will mend,
In embers bright, God is our friend.

Through tears that fall like gentle rain,
We learn to dance amidst the pain.
For in our grief, His love takes hold,
A refuge found in stories told.

The ashes whisper of the past,
Yet hope ignites, a flame that lasts.
In sorrow's arms, we rise and soar,
Refuge in strength, forevermore.

With every breath, we stand renewed,
In embers' glow, our faith imbued.
Though sorrow lingers, we will sing,
In anguish deep, His love will spring.

Constellations of Lost Devotion

In night's embrace, the stars align,
A tapestry of love divine.
For every heart that strayed away,
There lies a light to guide the way.

In constellations, stories weave,
A canvas bright for those who grieve.
Each flicker holds a vow once made,
In lost devotion, hope won't fade.

Through time and space, our spirits find,
The echoes of a love divine.
For every tear that fell in vain,
There shines a star to break the chains.

Though paths diverge, in twilight's glow,
The heart remembers what we know.
In every glance, a spark remains,
Constellations whisper love's refrains.

So gaze upon the sky so wide,
In lost devotion, love won't hide.
In every heart, a light survives,
Constellations hold our sacred lives.

Lamentations at the Pilgrim's Gate

In shadows deep, where silence weeps,
A weary heart on pathways steep.
With heavy load, the spirit sighs,
Beneath the gaze of endless skies.

Each footfall marked by grief and grace,
In searching for a sacred place.
Lost pleas ascend, like incense rise,
To find the solace where hope lies.

The gate stands firm, yet whispers call,
A promise held beyond the wall.
With trembling hands, the weary seek,
The strength to stand when spirits peak.

Through tears, the echoes sing of old,
Of stories shared, of truths retold.
In lamentations soft and clear,
The pilgrim's heart draws ever near.

So journey on, though burdens weigh,
The light will break, the night to fray.
At pilgrim's gate, where legends lay,
Find peace within the dawn of day.

Serpent and Dove in Distant Dreams

In realms unseen where shadows play,
The serpent coils, the dove holds sway.
Amidst the night, their whispers blend,
In tales of love that twist and bend.

With every breath, a choice is made,
In darkness bright, or light that fades.
The heart must choose between the two,
In every dream, the path rings true.

Through tempests fierce, the dove takes flight,
While serpent's form hides from the light.
In distant dreams, their dance unfolds,
A story woven, ancient, bold.

Yet in the clash of dark and dawn,
The sacred truth remains steadfast drawn.
For every wound that love has sewn,
The heart shall rise, no longer alone.

So heed the call within the night,
Where serpent speaks, and dove takes flight.
In distant dreams, the journey starts,
A sacred bond of joined hearts.

Lanterns amongst the Ashes

In a world of cinders, hope still glows,
With flickers bright where sorrow flows.
Lanterns shine through the darkened skies,
A beacon for the weary eyes.

Amongst the ashes, stories dwell,
Of broken dreams that once did swell.
Yet in the loss, the light remains,
As faith ignites amidst the pains.

Each lantern hung, a prayer sent high,
To mend the hearts that oft will cry.
With every flame, a tale reborn,
From out the fire, new life is torn.

Through silent nights, the spirits roam,
With guiding lights that call us home.
Though shadows loom and doubts eclipse,
The lanterns shine, our hope's eclipse.

So take the light and share it wide,
For in our hearts, the truth won't hide.
Amongst the ashes, evermore,
The lanterns shine, a sacred lore.

Revelations amidst Ruins

In crumbling walls, the whispers breathe,
Of ancient tales that never leave.
Each shattered stone holds heaven's sigh,
Revelations waiting, where spirits lie.

Beneath the rubble, truth unfolds,
In sacred ground, the past beholds.
With every crack, a light breaks through,
In ruins found, the heart renews.

The silence speaks, the echoes call,
To heed the lessons of the fall.
In whispered prayers, the dawn ignites,
Revelations born within the nights.

Amongst the dust, the visions arise,
A tapestry sewn of earth and skies.
Through all despair, a strength is found,
In brokenness, the hope profound.

So wander forth, through ruins bare,
With open hearts and souls laid bare.
For in the space where shadows play,
Revelations guide the weary way.

Seraphs in the Dust

Above, they soar with wings of light,
In shadows cast, they touch the night.
From heaven's grace, their whispers fall,
To lift the weary, to heed the call.

In humble earth, the seraphs tread,
Bearing burdens of the dead.
With every tear, a prayer is spun,
A dance of hope 'til day is done.

Their radiant eyes hold ancient wisdom,
In silent vows, they find the kingdom.
In the dust, they forge their path,
Embracing love, rejecting wrath.

Through valleys low, their voices ring,
To every heart, the promise bring.
In unity, our spirits blend,
With seraphs near, we shall transcend.

The Last Offering of a Wounded Heart

In shadows deep, my heart does ache,
A fragile gift, this love I make.
From broken dreams, I gather grace,
An offering in this sacred space.

Each tear that falls is but a prayer,
In whispered hopes, I lay them bare.
This wounded heart, a vessel sweet,
In agony, our souls will meet.

The altar stands, my feet are bare,
Upon it rests my silent prayer.
In love's lament, redemption calls,
With faith, I rise, though often I fall.

Through thorny paths, my spirit strays,
Yet in the dark, I find my ways.
With open arms, I face the night,
For in the pain, there blooms the light.

Etchings of an Enduring Hope

In distant skies, the stars entwine,
Each glimmer holds a story's line.
Etched in time, the dreams align,
A tapestry, divine design.

With every breath, a promise made,
In whispered winds, our fears allayed.
A luminous thread through darkened days,
In faith, our hearts shall find their ways.

From ashes rise, the phoenix soars,
With open hands, we knock on doors.
Each journey taken, a sacred thread,
In hope we tread where angels led.

Through trials faced, our spirits blend,
For love is strong, and never ends.
In unity, we walk as one,
With endless hope, our battles won.

The Spirit's Descent in Disarray

In the chaos, the spirit dives,
Through tangled thoughts, the essence thrives.
Fractured paths and broken seams,
In disarray, we chase our dreams.

With every fall, the roots grow deep,
In silence held, our secrets keep.
Through tumult clear, the light breaks free,
In shattered worlds, we learn to see.

The tempests rage, yet hearts remain,
In trials faced, we bear the pain.
In every storm, the spirit calls,
Through disarray, love never falls.

So let us dance in trembling light,
In radiant grace, we face the night.
For in each struggle, we find our way,
The spirit's strength will lead the day.

Penance in the Solitude

In silence deep, my soul does ache,
A whisper calls, for my heart's sake.
Beneath the stars, I hear the night,
In shadowed corners, I seek the light.

A restless mind, with burdens vast,
In moments still, I find the past.
Each breath a prayer, in solitude,
I cleanse my heart, renew my mood.

The wind it sighs, a gentle grace,
Reminding me of my sacred space.
With every tear, I seek to heal,
In penance found, my spirit feels.

The echoes pause, as dawn arrives,
A newfound strength within me thrives.
In tranquil lands, my sorrows wane,
I walk in faith, free from the chain.

In solitude, my heart's rebirth,
A hope rekindled, a promise worth.
Tomorrow waits, its light so bright,
I rise anew, embraced by light.

Relics of Reverence

In hallowed halls where shadows dance,
I find the remnants of a chance.
Each relic speaks, with quiet grace,
Of prayers and whispers that time can't erase.

The candle's glow, a beacon near,
Illuminates the sacred sphere.
With every flicker, stories unfold,
Of faith enduring and hearts bold.

Gilded frames with faces proud,
Of saints and sages, veiled in crowd.
In their embrace, I seek to stand,
To touch the sacred, to understand.

A chalice filled with dreams untold,
Carries whispers of the old.
In contemplation, my spirit grows,
With every relic, the truth bestows.

In reverent awe, I trace the line,
Of those who dared to seek divine.
Their legacy, a shining thread,
In every heart, their light is spread.

The Canvas of Hope

A canvas stretched before my eyes,
Where colors blend, and spirit flies.
With brush in hand, I paint the dawn,
Each stroke a dream, the darkness gone.

In hues of love, I craft my tale,
A journey worn, yet will prevail.
The palette whispers of grace anew,
In vibrant shades, my spirit grew.

The strokes of sorrow weave the light,
Transforming pain into pure sight.
With every shade, a lesson learned,
In faith's embrace, my heart now burned.

An artist's prayer upon the ground,
In joyful colors, hope is found.
The canvas wide, my heart laid bare,
In every layer, I find my prayer.

As twilight falls, the stars appear,
A masterpiece, my vision clear.
Each brushstroke sings, a life redeemed,
In hope reborn, my spirit beamed.

Crumbling Foundations of Faith

In ancient stones, I see the cracks,
Whispers of doubt, the heart it lacks.
Yet in this ruin, a seed remains,
A flicker small, through all the pains.

The walls may tremble, the roof may sway,
Yet in the struggle, I find my way.
With faith as mortar, I rebuild strong,
In trials faced, I know I belong.

Each tremor shakes my weary soul,
Yet through the chaos, I feel whole.
For in the ruins, truth will rise,
From crumbling faith, a spirit flies.

With every doubt, a lesson learned,
In every fall, a heart that yearned.
I'll stand amidst the falling stone,
For through this chaos, I am known.

In brokenness, there's beauty still,
A heart that's forged with iron will.
From crumbled ground, I'll lift my gaze,
And find in faith, my hope ablaze.

The Crossroads of Ash and Glory

At dusk where shadows linger long,
Two paths diverge, one weak, one strong.
The dust of ashes, whispers near,
Where glory's light can pierce the fear.

With every step, the heart must choose,
A road of hope or one to lose.
Through trials deep, in faith we walk,
For in our silence, we must talk.

The burdens heavy, yet spirits soar,
In moments lost, we seek for more.
With prayer as guide, we'll find our way,
To turn our night into the day.

Above the clouds, the heavens weep,
Yet through the pain, our souls will leap.
The crossroads blend both ash and light,
In grace, we rise, as dark takes flight.

From humble roots, new life will grow,
In every heart, His love will flow.
With courage strong, our fears we shed,
On ashes warm, we find our bed.

Incense Rising from the Despair

In shadows thick, where sorrows dwell,
A fragrant prayer begins to swell.
As incense drifts upon the air,
Our broken hearts, laid bare, in prayer.

With whispered hopes, we rise again,
From bitter loss to sweet refrain.
Each tear we shed becomes a song,
A hymn of faith where we belong.

Through stormy nights, our spirits yearn,
For solace found in every turn.
As thoughts ascend like smoke to skies,
Around us, love and peace arise.

The light of dawn breaks through the veil,
On wings of grace, our souls set sail.
In every trial, we find our strength,
As scents of hope fill every length.

A dance of light in darkness seen,
In depths of grief, the heart can glean.
That through despair, a spark ignites,
Incense rising, lifting lights.

Beneath the Broken Arch that Stands

Within the ruins, whispers trace,
A story held in time and space.
Beneath the arch, worn and grey,
Our dreams still dance, despite decay.

The echoes speak of battles fought,
Of all the lessons pain has taught.
With courage found in history,
We tread anew, our spirits free.

Each stone a testament to grace,
In shadows deep, we find our place.
The broken arch, a symbol clear,
Of hope that sits, despite the fear.

Through every crack, the light will seep,
In dusty corners, secrets keep.
With faith as guide, we move ahead,
To build anew where dreams have led.

Beneath the arch, we gather round,
In unity, our hearts are bound.
In brokenness, we find our worth,
To rise again, in love and mirth.

The Silent Hymn of the Forgotten

In quiet corners, hearts reside,
The whispers soft, where pain can hide.
A silent hymn, the soul's lament,
In shadows cast, our lives are spent.

Yet hope can rise from deep despair,
In every breath, a silent prayer.
Where voices fade, the heart still sings,
Of love, of loss, and all it brings.

For in the stillness, wisdom grows,
The hidden path where kindness flows.
Each soul remembered, every tale,
The silent hymn shall never fail.

In darkest nights, a light remains,
The warmth of love amidst the pains.
With every note, the past bestowed,
To kindle fire in pathways flowed.

So let us pause, embrace the still,
For in the quiet, hearts can fill.
The silent hymn of all who've gone,
A testament that love lives on.

Grace in the Grief

In shadows deep, His light will shine,
A whisper of hope, in sorrow's design.
With each tear shed, a sacrifice made,
His love lifts us up, never to fade.

Through valleys of heartache, we wander slow,
Yet in our despair, His mercy will flow.
In moments of silence, His presence we feel,
Revealing the truths that time cannot conceal.

From every burden, there's solace we yearn,
In faith's gentle hands, our spirits can learn.
Through trial and turmoil, His promise rings clear,
Grace in our grief, forever held dear.

The beauty in loss, a canvas of grace,
Each memory cherished, time can't erase.
In the arms of the Savior, we find our release,
In grief's tender song, we discover our peace.

Remnants of the Sacred

Amidst the ruins where shadows play,
The remnants of hope begin to sway.
In echoes of prayer that rise to the skies,
The sacred whispers, through hearts that cry.

In the ashes of doubt, His promise remains,
A tapestry woven in joy and in pains.
With every heartbeat, He gathers the lost,
In the fabric of faith, we embrace the cost.

Down paths of despair, His footprints we trace,
In the wilds of anguish, we seek His grace.
From the depths of sorrow, our spirits will soar,
Finding strength in the sacred, forevermore.

Through trials we face, in darkness we stand,
The remnants unfold, guided by His hand.
In brokenness, beauty, the light will unveil,
The sacred within, where love will prevail.

The Hymn of Forgotten Blessings

In silence we gather, lost in the past,
A hymn of remembrance, echoing steadfast.
For blessings bestowed, in shadows we tread,
With gratitude whispered, for all that we've shed.

Through laughter and heartache, our stories intertwine,
In the book of our lives, His light will define.
Each page tells a journey, a treasure we keep,
The hymn of our blessings, in silence we weep.

When storms rage around us, we raise up our song,
In the arms of His mercy, we know we belong.
Though forgotten by times, these blessings will stay,
A cadence of love that won't fade away.

In moments of doubt, when the world feels so wide,
We look for the blessings, and hope will abide.
In the depths of our souls, His grace reverberates,
A hymn of forgotten, where faith celebrates.

After the Fire: A Holy Reflection

In the aftermath, where embers lay bare,
We seek for the signs of a love still there.
From ashes of trials, new life will arise,
In the glow of the dawn, we find our reprise.

Like trees that withstand, we bend but don't break,
In reflections of ruin, new paths we will make.
Through the lens of the fire, our purpose we see,
Each trial a blessing, a chance to be free.

The sparks of creation ignite in the night,
With faith as our flame, guiding us to light.
The sacred rebirth, a testament strong,
After the fire, we learn to belong.

So let us remember, in darkness, we grow,
In every heartache, a seed we will sow.
After the fire, His love is our guide,
In holy reflections, forever abide.

The Vessel of Remembrance and Redemption

In the quiet heart of darkness,
A whisper calls, a sacred light.
For every sin and lost direction,
A vessel holds the hope in sight.

From ashes rise the seeds of mercy,
In tears, the sacred truth unfolds.
The broken find their peace in longing,
Within the grace that love upholds.

Each prayer a ripple in the stillness,
Each thought a beacon, shining bright.
For in the storm, we seek our shelter,
In the vessel, our souls take flight.

Together, we embrace the fire,
With faith, our spirits intertwine.
Through trials faced, we find our purpose,
In love's deep warmth, the stars align.

The road is long, the journey winding,
Yet in our hearts, we carry hope.
With every step, beside us guiding,
The vessel holds our souls to cope.

Sanctity in the Wake of Chaos

Amidst the storms that rattle foundations,
A calm resides, a whispered peace.
From shattered dreams, we find our solace,
In chaos, love does never cease.

When shadows dance upon the waters,
And hearts are frail with doubt and fear,
We rise like dawn from silent slumber,
With faith, we chase the shadows near.

The world may break with wild abandon,
Yet in our souls, a strength is sown.
For every tear, a hand extended,
In chaos, we are never alone.

Through fervent prayers and nightly vigils,
We hold the light, dispelling night.
In every struggle, find your courage,
For sacred paths will lead us right.

We walk as one through trials written,
In silence, hear creation's song.
In sanctity, our hearts united,
Embrace the grace that makes us strong.

Echoed Litanies in the Abyss

In the depths where shadows gather,
A song of hope begins to rise.
Echoed litanies of remembrance,
Illuminate the starless skies.

The void may whisper of confusion,
Yet still, our spirits find their cry.
For love transcends the bleakest inches,
Within the dark, our hopes will fly.

With every breath, we chant our longing,
Each syllable a bridge to light.
In the abyss, our faith unyielding,
Together, we reclaim the night.

The clouds may linger thick and heavy,
Yet within the heart, a flame does glow.
In unity, we sing our freedom,
Through every storm, our courage flows.

So raise your voice amidst the silence,
Let echoes form a sacred chorus.
In litanies, we'll find our solace,
Our souls entwined, forever glorious.

Signs of Grace in the Lonesome Night

In the lonesome night, a flicker glimmers,
A sign of grace amidst the shade.
With every heartbeat, love remembers,
The promises that never fade.

The stars above like guides of wisdom,
In distant fields, their light we seek.
For every path leads us to grace,
In moments soft, when hearts feel weak.

Through quiet prayers, we find our solace,
In solitude, a blessing lies.
For in the stillness, truth awakens,
And hope's embrace unbound the ties.

With every tear, a sign of healing,
In every wound, a glimpse of dawn.
The night may whisper of despair,
Yet faith can sing when all seems gone.

So rest your heart and trust the journey,
In lonesome nights, our spirits bloom.
For signs of grace will weave together,
A tapestry of love in room.

Carriers of the Unseen Light

In shadows deep, the whispers glow,
A spark divine, we come to know.
With hearts aglow, we bear the flame,
Through silent paths, we praise His name.

With every breath, the spirit sings,
The unseen grace of holy things.
We tread the earth, yet soar above,
As carriers of the boundless love.

In trials faced, our faith will stand,
Like gentle waves upon the sand.
With open arms, we greet the light,
As dawn breaks forth from velvet night.

With every step, the truth unfolds,
The ancient tales, forever told.
In unity, we find our place,
As one with Him, we seek His face.

So let us walk this sacred way,
Through shadows cast by yesterday.
In joy, in peace, our spirits rise,
Carriers of the unseen skies.

Blessings in the Afterglow

In golden hues, the sun does fall,
A tapestry that speaks to all.
In silent prayers, our hopes ascend,
As life unfolds, our hearts shall mend.

With whispers sweet of love and grace,
We seek the light in every place.
Through trials faced, our spirits grow,
In blessings found in afterglow.

The stars align, the night reveals,
In quiet trust, our fate it seals.
We gather strength from souls long past,
Their wisdom guides as shadows cast.

In every breath, the sacred calls,
As nature's song encompasses all.
With every heartbeat, life shall show,
The blessings found in afterglow.

So raise your voice and lift your eyes,
To skies that stretch in endless ties.
In gratitude, our spirits fly,
In love's embrace, we'll never die.

The Unraveling of the Celestial

A dance of stars, a cosmic play,
In mysteries, we find our way.
The heavens whisper softly low,
As truths emerge in sacred flow.

With every breath, the worlds collide,
In silent realms where dreams abide.
The galaxies sing their ancient song,
While time reveals where we belong.

As constellations weave their art,
The stories of the soul impart.
In twilight's hue, our hearts ignite,
The unraveling of the celestial light.

With every tear, a star lets fall,
The beauty found in sorrow's call.
In the vastness, a spark remains,
The echo of our joy and pains.

So let us journey through the night,
Embrace the dark to find the light.
In cosmic threads, our fates entwine,
In the sacred dance, we'll be divine.

Fading Joys of the Once-Believers

In echoes faint, the laughter dims,
A choir lost in faded hymns.
The candle's glow begins to wane,
As hearts once bold now know the pain.

The sacred trust begins to shake,
In whispered doubts, the silence wakes.
Once fiery souls, now shadows cast,
The fading joys of moments past.

In memories sweet, the light remains,
Yet burdens heavy, filled with chains.
The faith once strong, now flickers low,
In search of hope, we yearn to grow.

But within the sorrow, grace does dwell,
A gentle hand, a whispered spell.
In pain, we seek the light anew,
To find the path that once was true.

So let us gather, hearts in hand,
Together rise, together stand.
Though fading joys may touch our soul,
In love's embrace, we can be whole.

Parables of the Shattered Heart

In shadows deep where sorrows dwell,
A heart once whole now tells its tale,
In broken pieces, grace can swell,
In every sigh, God's love prevails.

Amidst the ruins, whispers rise,
Lessons learned through tearful eyes,
Each fragment sings of hope's reprise,
In shattered forms, the spirit flies.

Beneath the weight of worldly fears,
Resilience blooms through fallen tears,
The heart, though cracked, still perseveres,
In sacred truth, its song endears.

In emptiness, a light ignites,
Reviving dreams through endless nights,
The shattered heart, a beacon bright,
In every loss, a glimmer of might.

So gather round, O weary souls,
From brokenness, a story unfolds,
In shattered hearts, the truth consoles,
Divine redemption, love beholds.

Requiem for the Faithful

In silent prayers, the faithful weep,
For those who've crossed on journeys deep,
In solemn chants, their spirits keep,
The echoes of love, forever seep.

A candle's flame, a guiding light,
Through darkest paths, they took their flight,
In every heart, their souls ignite,
With whispered words, they change the night.

Remembering lives with grace adorned,
In every smile, their love reborn,
They paved the way, our spirits worn,
In hearts they linger, never scorned.

So let us raise our voices high,
In harmony with the heavenly sigh,
For every soul, we bid goodbye,
With faith's embrace, we hold the sky.

O faithful hearts, endure the pain,
Through loss, we find our hope again,
In every tear, love's sweet refrain,
In unity, we break the chain.

Faithfulness in the Fragments

In scattered pieces, life takes form,
Through trials faced, the spirit's warm,
In faithfulness, we weather storms,
Embracing grace, the heart transforms.

The fractured path reveals the truth,
In every age, in every youth,
A tapestry of faith, in sooth,
In fragments lost, still finds its ruth.

From brokenness, our strength is found,
In every scar, the love unbound,
In quiet whispers, hope is crowned,
In faithfulness, our hearts resound.

So gather close, O weary hearts,
From shattered dreams, a new life starts,
Embrace the journey, take your parts,
In pieces, joy and peace imparts.

Through every trial, our spirits soar,
In unity, we seek the core,
The faithful stand, forevermore,
In fragments bloom, our truth restore.

The Promise of a New Dawn

When night descends, the world feels cold,
A promise gleams, a tale retold,
In silence deep, the heart grows bold,
With every breath, new dreams unfold.

The sun will rise, dispelling fears,
No tear remains, no cloud appears,
In dawn's embrace, the heart endears,
With every ray, hope reappears.

In whispered prayers, the world awaits,
For second chances, open gates,
Through shadows past, love reinstates,
In every heart, the spirit resonates.

So let us walk with faith anew,
In paths of light, in love so true,
With every dawn, our spirits grew,
The promise kept, in all we pursue.

In mornings bright, joy's song we sing,
With every breath, our voices ring,
In the new dawn, our hearts take wing,
In faith's embrace, we rise and spring.

Genesis Amidst the Graveyards

In shadows deep, where silence speaks,
The whispers of the ancients rise.
Each stone a tale, each breath a dream,
Hope dawns anew beneath the skies.

Amidst the graves, we kneel in prayer,
A seed of faith in broken ground.
From dust to life, the spirit's flare,
In every heart, salvation found.

The echo of the olden hymn,
Transforms the night into the day.
With every tear, the light grows dim,
Yet love persists, will find a way.

From ashes born, the soul shall rise,
In unity, we lift our sight.
For in the dark, the promise lies,
A resurrection in the night.

With every grave, a story told,
Of faith that conquers, love that thrives.
In graveyards vast, the truth unfolds,
For life eternal, our heart drives.

The Last Prayer of the Wandering Spirit

Beneath the stars, the spirit roams,
In search of peace, a sacred space.
Yet longing echoes in the gloams,
For solace found in love's embrace.

The final prayer drifts with the breeze,
A whispered hope for tranquil skies.
In nights of doubt, in fervent pleas,
The heart finds strength and never dies.

Through valleys deep, the shadows cast,
The journey long, yet faith does steer.
Each step is woven, shadows past,
With every heartbeat, truth draws near.

In silence, light breaks through the dark,
Compassion blooms in restless hearts.
The night is still, but love's the spark,
As wandering souls find where hope starts.

So let the spirit find its rest,
In tranquil light, where peace aligns.
For in the end, we are most blessed,
United in love, life intertwines.

Foundations of Faith in a Shattered World

In ruins lies our weary plight,
Yet from the rubble, hope takes flight.
Though storms may rage, the spirit stands,
With faith anew, our hearts in hands.

Each shattered stone, a prayer raised,
In unity, our souls ablaze.
For in the struggle, truth is found,
As love emerges from the ground.

The darkest hour, a child's sweet cry,
A testament as time goes by.
Through trials faced, we rise once more,
The light of faith, our steady core.

With every tear that carves our path,
The grace of God upholds our wrath.
Though broken dreams may haunt the night,
The dawn will come to bring us light.

So stand together, firm and bold,
With hands entwined, our story told.
In every heart, the promise knits,
Foundations strong, our spirit fits.

Threads of Divinity in the Tattered

In fabric torn, the thread still gleams,
With every stitch, a hope redeems.
Though life may fray at edges worn,
In sacred light, new dreams are born.

Each moment shared, a silken strand,
Woven by grace, by love's own hand.
Though storms may rage and shadows creep,
In faith we find the strength to leap.

Through trials faced, the spirit glows,
In tattered cloth, the beauty grows.
For even in the darkest hour,
The threads of love reveal their power.

With every tear, a story weaves,
Of hope revived, of truth that cleaves.
In every heart, a bond entwined,
In threaded hearts, divinity finds.

So take the scraps that life has sown,
And find the grace in every tone.
For in the tattered, life will gleam,
In threads of faith, we dare to dream.

Sanctuaries of Lost Souls

In shadows deep, the weary find,
A refuge softly intertwined.
In whispered prayers, their hopes arise,
Bold faith ignites beneath dark skies.

The path is fraught with tears and sighs,
Yet light breaks forth, a sweet surprise.
A gentle hand to guide them through,
To sacred ground where love is true.

In sacred halls where echoes dwell,
They share their burdens, hearts compel.
The promise blooms, a flower bright,
As lost souls gather in the night.

With every step, redemption calls,
Through open gates, the spirit sprawls.
In delicate grace, they stand aligned,
In sanctuaries, their souls combined.

And faith becomes their tether strong,
A hymn of hope, a sacred song.
Together, they defend the light,
In holy bonds that conquer night.

Pilgrims in the Wasteland

Through barren lands, the pilgrims stride,
With dust of ages as their guide.
In search of truth, they seek the grace,
To find a holy, sacred place.

Each step a prayer, each breath a song,
In quiet faith, they move along.
Their burdens shared, their spirits rise,
In unity beneath vast skies.

The sun may scorch, the night may chill,
Yet hearts ablaze, they seek the thrill.
For in the stillness, wisdom calls,
In wasteland's grip, the spirit sprawls.

With weary hands and weary feet,
They journey forth, no place elite.
Yet in each trial, they find the hand,
Of grace bestowed upon the sand.

For in the desert's cruel embrace,
They hear the echoes of His grace.
Through trials faced and storms unfurled,
They find their light within the world.

Beneath the Gaze of the Silent Stars

Beneath the vast and velvet night,
The stars ignite with gentle light.
In silence deep, lost souls appear,
Their whispered dreams, a song sincere.

With every glance, the heavens speak,
In cosmic sweep, they seek the weak.
A tapestry of fate unwinds,
As faith entwines with heart and mind.

In quietude, the travelers learn,
Through shadowed paths, their spirits yearn.
And in the dark, a spark ignites,
A beacon shining, guiding nights.

The galaxy, a soothing balm,
Restores the weary, grants them calm.
In every heart, a star takes flight,
A promise born within the night.

So let them gaze and let them dream,
For through the stars, the spirit beams.
United in this cosmic dance,
They find their hope, their second chance.

Chronicles of the Wandering Spirit

In tales of old, the spirits roam,
With every path, they seek a home.
The whispers linger in the air,
Awakening hearts in deep despair.

Through valleys low and mountains high,
They tread where hopes and sorrows lie.
Each journey paints the soul's delight,
In chronicles of endless night.

With every step, a story spun,
Of battles fought and victories won.
In ancient echoes, wisdom's lore,
Unfolds the truth, forevermore.

As wandering spirits find their way,
Through darkness deep, both night and day.
They carry faith, a woven thread,
In sacred texts, the spirit's shed.

And in those tales, the heart awakens,
To deeper truths, forever shaken.
Transcending pain, they shall ascend,
In chronicles where shadows blend.

The Veil of Forgotten Trust

In shadows deep, the whispers wane,
A promise lost, a lingering pain.
The heart once bold, now cloaked in fear,
Calls for the light, for hope to appear.

With faith as shield, we tread the night,
Where doubts arise, extinguish light.
Yet in the silence, a echo calls,
Restoring peace when the heart stumbles and falls.

Beneath the veil, redemption breathes,
A tender hand that gently weaves.
Through trials faced, a path unfolds,
In every tear, a truth that holds.

Let not the burden weigh thee down,
For in His grace, wear glory's crown.
The veil may tear, the dawn may break,
Reviving trust, as morning wakes.

In every whisper, a promise found,
A sacred bond in love unbound.
Lift thy gaze, embrace the trust,
For in His light, we rise from dust.

Elements of a Fractured Sanctuary

In the temple's heart, shadows creep,
Where silence haunts, the spirits weep.
The stones are cracked, yet still they stand,
An echo of faith held in trembling hands.

Winds of doubt through cracks do flow,
Chilling the marrow, seeding woe.
Yet in the storm, a candle glows,
Guiding the lost to sacred throes.

The altar bears the marks of strife,
In every wound, a tale of life.
Yet hope as rain falls from the skies,
Restoring faith where the spirit flies.

Each prayer sung, a balm for scars,
Lifting the gaze to distant stars.
In each element, the divine's embrace,
Awakening hearts in this fractured place.

From ashes rise a trust profound,
In brokenness, new hope is found.
For in the cracks, the light comes through,
Revealing paths where faith renews.

Prayers of the Unanswered

In hushed repose, the voice of night,
Calls out in longing for sacred light.
Hearts heavy laden with silent pleas,
Whispers rise high on trembling knees.

The skies remain, a canvas gray,
Where souls seek solace, but shadows play.
Yet even here, the spirit weeps,
In trust divine, the promise keeps.

With every sigh, a question borne,
In the echoes of hope, where dreams are worn.
Yet still we seek, with hearts aglow,
In the darkest hours, love's tender flow.

The unanswered prayers wade deep as seas,
Yet in the silence comes sacred ease.
Each tear that falls, a spark ignites,
Showing the way through endless nights.

For in the void, love's whispers stay,
Teaching the soul how to find the way.
In the unanswered, we learn to trust,
Finding God's grace in the cosmic dust.

Serenity in the Storm's Eye

As thunder rolls, and shadows blend,
A tranquil heart finds time to mend.
In chaos bound, a stillness grows,
Bringing peace that gently flows.

The whirlwind roars, yet I remain,
Within the tempest, beyond the pain.
A lighthouse beams, a guiding star,
Reminding me of how loved we are.

In every gust, His presence sown,
Stronger still when all seems blown.
Amidst the storm, an inner calm,
A refuge found, a soothing balm.

With every wave, I rise, I sway,
Trusting the path, come what may.
For in this eye where stillness lies,
Divine embrace, the spirit flies.

When storms shall pass, the dawn will break,
Renewed in spirit, we rise, awake.
In tranquility's heart, we claim our place,
Serenity found in His endless grace.

Tapestry of the Unseen

In stillness, whispers weave the thread,
A tapestry of love, when hope is spread.
Each heart a stitch in divine design,
Unseen hands guide us, eternally align.

Stars reflect in the waters below,
As secrets of faith in silence grow.
With every dawn, the patterns renew,
A sacred dance, old and ever true.

Through valleys deep, where shadows loom,
The light breaks forth, dispelling gloom.
In every tear, a pearl of grace,
Together we rise, in His embrace.

Each moment crafted, His will unfolds,
In the fabric of life, the heart's song holds.
With gratitude, we honor our place,
A vibrant thread in eternal grace.

So let us walk, hand in hand we go,
Embracing the mystery, the love we sow.
For in our journey, the unseen gleams,
A radiant tapestry woven in dreams.

Ascension from Shadows

Lift your gaze, for dawn is near,
From shadowed paths, we conquer fear.
Each step we take, a whispered prayer,
Guided by light, with love to share.

Release the chains that hold you tight,
Embrace the warmth of holy light.
In darkness, hope begins to glow,
A spark ignites, in hearts we sow.

Through trials faced and sorrows shared,
The spirit rises, steadfast, prepared.
With wings of faith, we soar above,
A testament of grace and love.

In unity, our voices blend,
As angels rally, their song extend.
Together we rise, from depths profound,
In sacred trust, our strength is found.

So lift your heart and sing with me,
In every note, we set love free.
For from the shadows, we ascend high,
With faith our beacon, we touch the sky.

Grace Unwound in Time

In the stillness of a moment's grace,
Timeless whispers find their place.
Each tick of the clock, a sacred call,
Unraveling truths that bind us all.

Through ages past, the stories flow,
In every heartbeat, the Spirit's glow.
Each lesson learned, a step refined,
In the fabric of time, our souls aligned.

Like rivers run and seasons change,
In grace we stretch, in love we range.
Each moment breathing, a gift divine,
In every heartbeat, His love align.

So let us dance beneath the sky,
With hearts unbound, and spirits high.
In the sacred circle, we are entwined,
A melody of hope, forever aligned.

As time unwinds, we find our way,
With grace enfolding, come what may.
In unity we trust, in love we climb,
Together we shine, through grace and time.

A New Covenant of Light

In the dawning of a new refrain,
A promise whispered through joy and pain.
Hearts entwined, a covenant strong,
In every breath, we find our song.

With open skies, and spirits unshackled,
Each moment blessed, our hope unstrangled.
Through trials faced, our spirits soar,
United in faith, forevermore.

A tapestry woven with threads of trust,
In every heart, a spark of lust.
A journey shared, hand in hand we tread,
A sacred bond, where angels dare to spread.

So let us gather, in light we stand,
Together we rise, across this land.
In gratitude, we embrace the night,
For dawn shall break, a new covenant of light.

With every heartbeat, let love ignite,
For in our unity, we shine so bright.
A new beginning unfolds in grace,
A sacred promise, an eternal space.

Covenant of the Survivors

In the shadow of the ruins, they stand,
Holding fast with trembling hand.
A whisper of promises, strong and clear,
Guiding the lost to draw near.

The breath of the ancients fills the air,
With prayers spoken in deep despair.
Together, their spirits rise and soar,
A bond eternal, forevermore.

Through trials and storms, they find their way,
In unity, they learn to stay.
With hearts entwined, a sacred trust,
In the soil of sorrow, hope turns to dust.

Each tear a testament of resolve,
In the light of love, they dissolve.
As branches reach for the skies above,
They cultivate resilience and love.

Through the echoes of time, they carry on,
With the strength of many and the will of one.
The covenant renewed with every prayer,
In the silent promise, their souls laid bare.

Seraphim Weep for the Fallen

High in the heavens, the seraphim cry,
For souls lost in shadows, drifting by.
With wings like flames and eyes of grace,
They mourn the smiles that time can't replace.

From the heights they soar, a sorrowful song,
Calling the faithful to right the wrong.
In circles of light, their voices blend,
A chorus of loss that will never end.

In the silence of night, their tears cascade,
Weaving a tapestry where hope won't fade.
Each droplet of grief, a sacred plea,
To guide the weary, to set them free.

Yet amidst the pain, a promise ignites,
In shadows they share the celestial lights.
With every heartbeat, the fallen are kissed,
In realms above, they coexist.

For those who have gone, a vigil they keep,
In the heart of the seraphim, love runs deep.
Through the veil of sorrow, they find the way,
To honor the fallen, to light their stay.

The Garden of Regret and Revival

In the garden where shadows intertwine,
Regrets bloom under the weight of time.
With petals of sorrow, the memories unfold,
Yet whispers of revival begin to take hold.

The soil is rich with the tears that fall,
Each drop a testament to love's quiet call.
From ashes to blossoms, the cycle runs deep,
In the arms of renewal, the spirits leap.

Where once there was darkness, the light breaks through,
Painting the canvas with hues ever new.
In fragrant embrace, the past finds its peace,
As the garden of hearts learns to release.

With each dawn that rises, the cycles renew,
The dance of forgiveness, forever in view.
In the mingling of joy and the ache of regret,
Lies the fullness of life that we won't forget.

Amongst the thorns, the wildflowers grow,
A testament to healing, a sacred flow.
In the garden of hope, we nurture our souls,
As together we journey, as one, we are whole.

Hymns of Hope in the Darkened Skies

When shadows gather and light grows dim,
The heart unites in a sacred hymn.
Voices rise like incense to the night,
Calling forth courage, igniting the light.

With each whispered prayer, the dark bids adieu,
Faith shines brighter with each gaze anew.
The stars, they listen, as souls intertwine,
In the depths of despair, their spirits align.

Through valleys of sorrow, they boldly tread,
In the arms of love, they find their stead.
With every heartbeat, a story begins,
Of triumph and grace where hope always wins.

For every tear that falls, a promise awaits,
With faith as our guide, we're free from our fates.
In the hymn of the brave, a chorus rings true,
Together we stand, and together renew.

In darkened skies where the world feels lost,
Hymns of hope echo, no matter the cost.
In unity's strength, we rise from the plight,
With love as our lantern, we welcome the light.

Shadows of Grace at Dusk

In evening's hush, the shadows stretch wide,
Where whispers of faith and hope abide.
Soft prayers ascend to the starry dome,
In twilight's grace, we find our home.

The glow of dreams under the fading light,
Sustains the weary in their plight.
With each heartbeat, a promise unfolds,
In the quiet, divine tales are told.

The breeze carries hymns from the trees,
Gentle reminders, as sweet as these.
In every sigh, a sacred embrace,
We walk the path, shadows of grace.

As dusk descends on the world anew,
A calming peace seeps through and through.
In every flicker, a chance to mend,
Each moment shared, a love to extend.

So let us gather at the close of day,
In unity, we find our way.
With hearts aglow in the soft twilight,
Together we shine, a beacon of light.

The Light that Lingers in the Ruins

Amid the rubble and fallen stone,
The remnants of faith have quietly grown.
In broken places, the heart still beats,
A flicker of hope where despair retreats.

Through shattered walls, the sun spills gold,
Whispering secrets that time has told.
Each crack reveals a story of grace,
In the ruins, we find our place.

The echoes of prayers long sung,
Still gently rise on the lips of the young.
In every tear, a lesson learned,
In every loss, the heart still yearned.

From ashes to light, a journey made,
From darkness to dawn, fears will fade.
In the remnants, His presence shines,
A testament forged across the lines.

The light that lingers, forever stays,
Guiding our steps through winding ways.
In the ruins, we claim our right,
To rebuild and bask in the radiant light.

Psalms Written in the Dust

In the shifting sands, a psalm unfolds,
Whispers of wisdom, ancient and bold.
Each grain a story of trials faced,
In the dust, eternity embraced.

With every breath, we etch and weave,
Lessons of love that we believe.
The fragile thread of every life,
Woven in songs of joy and strife.

From ashes to dawn, the voices rise,
Carrying hope to the endless skies.
In the quiet moments, the soul finds peace,
In the stillness, distractions cease.

The dust bears witness to every tear,
A testament for the world to hear.
In humble prayers, our hearts aligned,
The sacred echoes, perfectly timed.

So let us write on the canvas bare,
As psalms of dust fill the air.
In every footprint, a story told,
In Christ's embrace, we are consoled.

Miracles Born from the Fractured

In shattered places, grace is found,
In brokenness, the soul is crowned.
From cracks of pain, the light can pour,
Miracles rise from the fractured floor.

With every wound, a story to tell,
In trials faced, we learn to dwell.
Each scar a marker of battles fought,
In struggle and strength, our spirits caught.

In the depths of sorrow, we seek the bright,
Finding beauty within the night.
In each tear shed, a rainbow springs,
Through pain, the heart learns to sing.

So let us cherish the pieces we bear,
For in the cracks, Divinity's care.
With faith as our guide, we mend and weave,
In our brokenness, we truly believe.

Miracles bloom where hope is sown,
In the fractured, we will find our own.
Through every fall, we rise anew,
In love's embrace, the miracles grew.

Echoes of Redemption's Dawn

In the quiet of morning light,
Hope rises on wings of prayer,
Forgiveness weaves through the night,
A fragrant promise fills the air.

With shadows fading into grace,
Hearts awaken, souls set free,
The dawn reveals a sacred space,
Where love's embrace is meant to be.

Each tear shed, a seed of trust,
In barren soil, redemption grows,
From ashes born, we rise from dust,
To wear the crown that mercy shows.

With every step, we walk the path,
Guided by the light above,
In the stillness, we escape wrath,
Wrapped tightly in the arms of love.

As echoes fade into the morn,
Our spirits sing in sweet refrain,
From brokenness, we all are torn,
But from this pain, we find our gain.

The Altar of Regrets

Upon the stones of sorrow lay,
The weight of past, unspoken dreams,
With heavy hearts, we search for day,
Where grace can mend our frayed seams.

Each whispered prayer, a cry for peace,
As lanterns flicker in the night,
From the depths, we seek release,
To find within the path to light.

We build our altar, made of tears,
With memories etched in every word,
Time becomes a thread of fears,
But hope still sings, though seldom heard.

Forgiveness stands where shadows pause,
Inviting us to breathe anew,
In sacred stillness, we find cause,
To turn our hearts and listen true.

So let the past no longer bind,
With every heartbeat, we move on,
In love and faith, anew we find,
The strength to rise with every dawn.

Beneath the Silence of Broken Prayers

In the stillness, whispers clear,
With every sigh, a heart laid bare,
Beneath the silence, love draws near,
In aching void, we find our prayer.

Each word unspoken haunts the night,
As dreams and fears entwine as one,
Yet in this darkness, hope takes flight,
Embracing grace like morning sun.

Shattered moments, pieces lost,
Yet faith remains, a steady guide,
In every trial, we count the cost,
And find the strength to turn the tide.

With every heartache, love is sown,
In barren ground, a garden blooms,
From broken prayers, new seeds are grown,
As light dispels the darkest glooms.

So let our silence be a song,
A melody of hope and trust,
For in this journey, we belong,
Awakening from dreams, we must.

Whispers from the Ruins of Grace

In the ruins where shadows lie,
Soft whispers rise to greet the dawn,
Amidst the wreckage, dreams still fly,
In fragile hearts, new hope is drawn.

The echoes speak of love sustained,
Through trials faced and battles fought,
In every scar, a lesson gained,
In every tear, a glimpse of thought.

With open arms, the past we greet,
Forgiven sins, a healing balm,
In every loss, there's love complete,
In troubled waters, we find calm.

From ashes rise the stones of fate,
With every breath, we claim our place,
Uniting souls in love's estate,
The whispers weave a tapestry of grace.

So let the world hear every sound,
Of hope reborn in broken dreams,
For in our hearts, love's warmth is found,
And through the ruins, bright light beams.

Whispers of the Shattered Sanctuary

In shadows deep where silence clings,
A broken faith, the sorrow sings.
The echoes of our prayers resound,
In the rubble, lost hopes are found.

Divine light flickers, dim but true,
Guiding the hearts that start anew.
Amidst the ashes, spirits rise,
To weave their dreams, to touch the skies.

The altar cracked, yet love persists,
In fractured stones, the holy tryst.
Through whispered words and gentle pleas,
We find our way, our souls at ease.

From shattered walls, compassion flows,
In every heart, a garden grows.
Rekindled flames of grace ignite,
Restoring faith through darkest night.

Let every tear be washed away,
As dawn breaks forth, a brighter day.
In every shard, a chance to mend,
The sacred path, where love transcends.

Echoes of the Sacred Silence

In the stillness where spirits dwell,
A sacred hush, a hidden spell.
The quietude of thoughts divine,
Whispers secrets, pure and fine.

Each breath a prayer, a soft caress,
In silence deep, we find our rest.
The heart attuned to heaven's song,
Where souls belong, where we are strong.

Through shadowed realms, the echoes call,
In reverence, we rise, not fall.
With every heartbeat, grace bestowed,
In gentle tones, our path is showed.

The sacred silence speaks of peace,
In unity, our fears release.
A bond that weaves through night and day,
In tranquil hearts, our spirits sway.

Let every echo guide us near,
To realms of love, to angels' cheer.
In sacred silence, we abide,
With every step, the Lord our guide.

Beneath the Ruins of Reverence

Amidst the haze of twisted stone,
Lie whispers of the once well-known.
A sanctuary of faith now lost,
Yet hope survives, no matter the cost.

In every crack, the light breaks through,
Beneath the rubble, grace anew.
The remnants of a faith so bright,
Glow like stars in the endless night.

Through broken walls, the winds still sing,
Of ancient prayers and holy things.
Each fallen beam, a story told,
In valiant hearts, the truth unfolds.

From dusty floors, the spirits rise,
In fractured dreams, we recognize.
The strength of love that never fades,
In every loss, a gift cascades.

So let us gather, hand in hand,
In unity, a steadfast band.
Reviving dreams long laid to rest,
Beneath the ruins, we are blessed.

Remnants of the Divine Messenger

Upon the path where angels tread,
The remnants of the words once said.
In whispers soft, they guide us still,
To seek the light, to walk His will.

In every heart, a message dwells,
Of love profound, as truth compels.
Though storms may rage and shadows loom,
The light of faith will pierce the gloom.

In simple acts of kindness shown,
The messenger's grace is freely sown.
Through service given, lives we touch,
The echoes of His love mean much.

From every trial, a lesson learned,
The fire of faith forever burned.
In every struggle, hope is found,
The divine whispers all around.

So let us cherish every word,
In silence, let our hearts be stirred.
For in the remnants, truth remains,
A sacred path through joys and pains.

The Return of Lost Benedictions

In the silence of the night, we pray,
The whispers of grace call us back.
Lost blessings find their way to light,
Hearts awaken from their sacred lack.

Through shadows long, the sun breaks through,
Guiding us to paths divine.
In every tear, a promise new,
In every struggle, grace we find.

Hope rises like a morning star,
Embracing all who seek the truth.
With gentle hands, He heals the scar,
Restoring faith in hearts of youth.

We gather 'round the table's grace,
Sharing stories of love and light.
In every face, a holy space,
Where lost benedictions take flight.

And as we walk this blessed soil,
Our voices join a sacred song.
Through trials and the holy toil,
We find our place where we belong.

Echoes of a Hollow Psalm

In the stillness of the dawn, we weep,
For echoes of a psalm once sweet.
Voices linger, promises deep,
Yet hollow notes mark the retreat.

With every tear, a story's told,
Of faith that falters, hope that fades.
In silent prayers, our hearts unfold,
Searching for light in shadowed glades.

The hymn of life, a distant strain,
Resonates with dreams now lost.
Yet in our hearts, the truth remains,
That love endures despite the cost.

We rise and fall, like tides at sea,
Each note a step on paths unknown.
In the echoes, we seek to be,
Restored to grace, not all alone.

In quiet moments, we align,
With every breath, the hope we send.
The hollow psalm begins to shine,
As spirits mend and hearts transcend.

The Spirit's Cry after the Storm

After the tempest, calm descends,
Whispers of mercy, soft and kind.
The spirit's cry, a message sends,
In every heart, peace we find.

Through darkest nights and howling winds,
We learn the strength of quiet faith.
The storm may rage, but love transcends,
A bond unbroken, our hearts wraith.

In the aftermath, we stand renewed,
With courage born from trials past.
Each wound a testament of good,
To rise again, our spirits cast.

The skies once grey now glow with light,
Hope heralds a new day's embrace.
Together we take wing in flight,
Finding solace in love's grace.

Embrace the dawn; the storm has passed,
In every breath, hear wisdom's call.
The spirit sings, our souls amassed,
From brokenness, we rise, stand tall.

Rebirth in the Cradle of Sorrow

In the cradle where sorrows rest,
New life emerges from the pain.
Each tear a seed, a glorious test,
In darkness, light will break the chain.

From ashes cold, the spirit breathes,
With open arms, we learn to love.
In the depths, the heart still believes,
A whisper sent from heavens above.

Through valleys deep, we walk in grace,
Embracing shadows, shining bright.
For in sorrow's arms, we find a place,
Where hope and faith ignite the night.

In the rebirth, we shed our fears,
A phoenix rising from the ground.
In laughter shared, in loving tears,
Redemption's song will be our sound.

So cradle sorrow, let it bloom,
For life anew will soon break free.
In every heart, love's sweet perfume,
A token of our victory.

Milton Keynes UK
Ingram Content Group UK Ltd.
UKHW022223251124
451566UK00006B/99